the san juan islands

the san juan islands

Crown Jewels of the Pacific Coast

Mark Gardner

SASQUATCH BOOKS
SEATTLE

Cover: The skiff *Martha*, Camp Four Winds, Orcas Island.
Page 1: A commercial fisherman's tools. **Page 2**: A ferry slips past Brown Island, headed toward the landing at Friday Harbor.
Right: Upturned kayaks. **Page 6**: A ferry traverses San Juan Channel.

Printed in Singapore
Published by Sasquatch Books
Distributed in Canada by Raincoast Books, Ltd.
07 06 05 04 03 02 01 6 5 4 3 2 1

Cover and interior designer: Karen Schober
Copy editor: Don Roberts

Library of Congress Cataloging in Publication Data
Gardner, Mark, 1953–
The San Juan Islands : crown jewels of the Pacific Coast / by Mark Gardner
p. cm.
ISBN 1-57061-281-1
1. Natural history—Washington (State)—San Juan Islands. 2. San Juan Islands (Wash.)—History. I. Title.
QH105.W2 G37 2001
508.797'74—dc21 00-052262

Sasquatch Books
615 Second Avenue
Seattle, Washington 98104
(206) 467-4300
www.SasquatchBooks.com
books@SasquatchBooks.com

acknowledgments

As with any other project like this, many people helped me along the way. I thank Alan and Katie Barsamian, Larry Marx, Roger and Michelle Shober, Ron and Marci Kenny, Bill and Colleen Wright, Kevin Ranker, Larry and Deb McEdward, and the many other islanders who gave me ideas and suggestions; Art Wolfe, Ray Pfortner, and Chris Eckoff for their assistance and encouragement; Kate Rogers and Karen Schober at Sasquatch Books for turning a bunch of slides into this book; my son, Ben, for helping me in the field and sometimes driving the boat; and finally my wife, Dona Reed, for, well, just for everything.

dedication

This book is dedicated to all those people who work to preserve the San Juan Islands and the many other special places in the world. This book is my contribution to that cause.

crown jewels of the pacific coast

The morning fog lifts as the ferry enters the San Juan Islands through Thatcher Pass. Passengers on deck scan the waters ahead for an orca's spout or simply bask in the emerging sunshine. The islands seem to sparkle, dark-green jewels against a bright, blue sky. Even though I've traveled this route hundreds of time, I too become enthralled with the scenery and soon forget the book in front of me. A harbor seal surfaces near the ferry and watches us as intently as we watch him. Gulls soar in the ferry's slipstream. In the protected bays that we pass, yachts bob at anchor and commercial fishers check their traps for Dungeness crab. By the time the ferry lands, all on board are under the spell of the San Juan Islands.

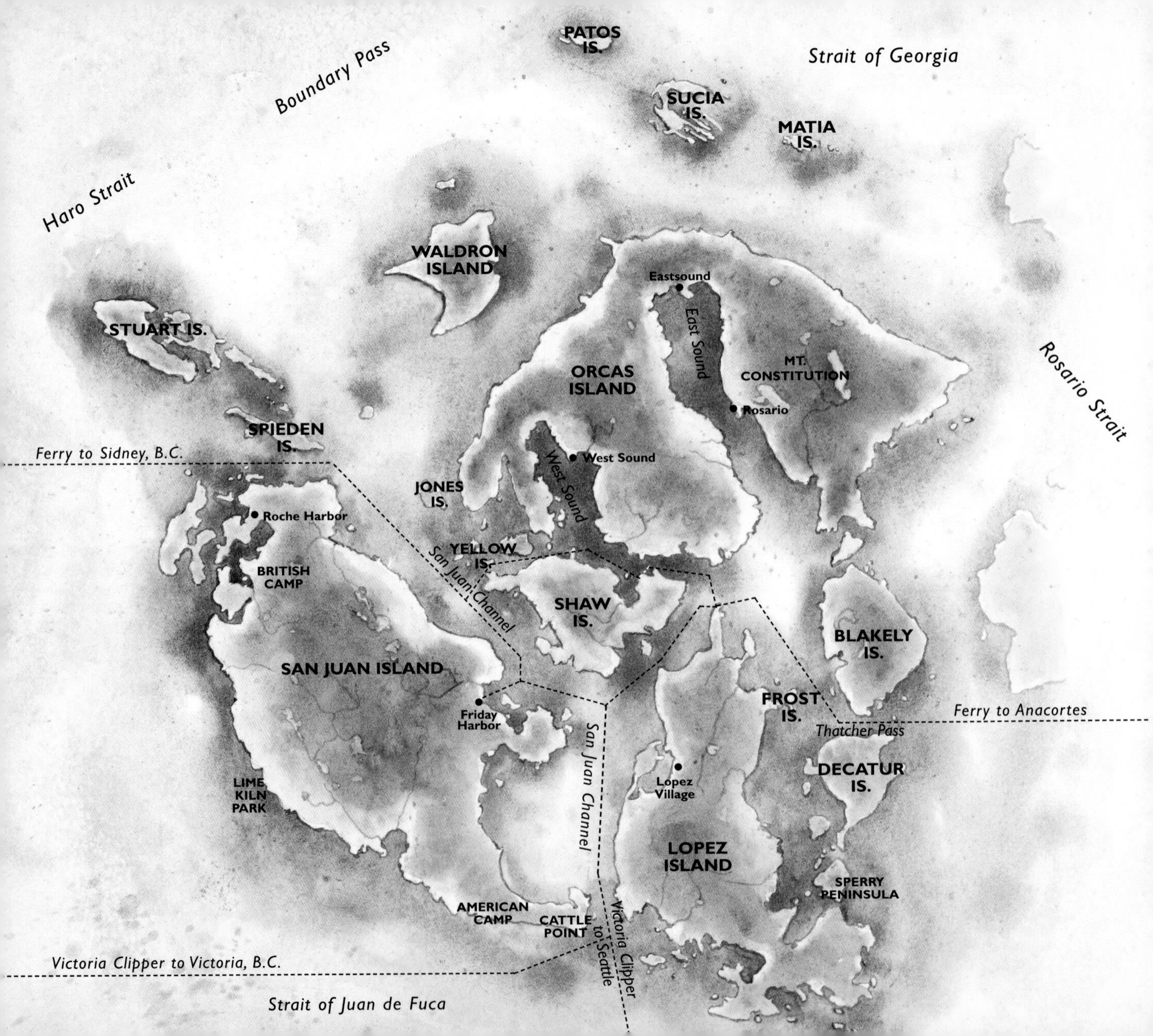

PATOS IS.
Strait of Georgia
Boundary Pass
SUCIA IS.
MATIA IS.
Haro Strait
WALDRON ISLAND
Eastsound
STUART IS.
East Sound
Rosario Strait
MT. CONSTITUTION
ORCAS ISLAND
Rosario
SPIEDEN IS.
Ferry to Sidney, B.C.
West Sound
West Sound
JONES IS.
Roche Harbor
YELLOW IS.
San Juan Channel
BRITISH CAMP
SHAW IS.
BLAKELY IS.
SAN JUAN ISLAND
FROST IS.
Friday Harbor
Ferry to Anacortes
Thatcher Pass
San Juan Channel
DECATUR IS.
Lopez Village
LIME KILN PARK
LOPEZ ISLAND
SPERRY PENINSULA
AMERICAN CAMP
CATTLE POINT
Victoria Clipper to Seattle
Victoria Clipper to Victoria, B.C.
Strait of Juan de Fuca

Reachable only by boat or plane, this magic archipelago of 172 islands is tucked into the northwest corner of the United States. The Canadian border lies just a few miles to the north and to the west. Counting rocks with names, the number of islands rises to more than 400. At a very low tide, another 300 or so emerge, many barely large enough to hold a basking seal. The San Juans are actually a small mountain chain that was created by uplift, carved by glaciers, and then mostly submerged, leaving only the tops of the chain's peaks and crags visible today.

Surrounded by waters cooled year-round by Pacific currents and lying in the rain shadow of the Olympic Mountains, the San Juans enjoy a temperate, often sunny, Mediterranean-type climate. Winters and springs are wet, but less so than on the mainland—the islands receive about half the annual rainfall of nearby Seattle. Summers and falls are dry, with weather more similar to that of California's central coast than the Pacific Northwest.

Their relatively dry climate, geologic youth, and isolation make the San Juans ecologically unique, and the variety of habitats—from marine waters to forested mountain slopes to open prairies—fosters a diverse assemblage. However, because the islands are isolated and relatively small, some animal species common on the mainland, such as large predators, are absent here.

The southern flanks of the islands are dominated by open prairies of tall grasses, wildflowers, and even prickly-pear cactus. Groves of Garry oak dot the same slopes, giving some areas a savannah-like appearance. Tree species common in other regions but unusual on the Northwest coast, such as juniper and aspen, grow throughout the islands. But perhaps the San Juans' most distinctive tree is the Pacific madrona, which grows in tall, often beautifully sculpted twists and turns. Madronas keep their thick, waxy leaves in winter and shed their outer bark to reveal a bright-red inner layer, which in turn peals away in summer, exposing the soft, green wood beneath.

The islands' forests were heavily logged in the late 1800s and early 1900s to supply timber for shipbuilding and fuel for limekilns. Today the islands have mostly recovered, with second-growth forests dominated by Douglas fir and an undergrowth of Oregon grape, salal, and wildflowers. A few stands of old-growth western redcedar and Douglas fir remain. The forests on the islands' upper slopes also include grand fir, western hemlock, and other subalpine trees.

With their diversity of habitat, the San Juans are rich in bird life. Great blue herons, oystercatchers, and a variety of other shorebirds live along the rocky coasts. Bald eagles, peregrine falcons, and other birds of prey are relatively common. On the open water, rhinoceros auklets, common murres, and even the endangered marbled murrelet bob and dive. Upland, feisty rufous hummingbirds feed on the wildflowers. Turkey vultures and harriers prowl above the prairies. Cooper's hawks patrol the forests, where you often hear the raven's *kronk* and the varied thrush's melodic call. The islands are also an important rest stop for birds migrating along the Pacific Flyway, so swans, phalaropes, and other nonresident species are common visitors during spring and fall.

The waters surrounding the islands teem with life. The orca, or killer whale, is at the top of the marine food chain. (The name "killer whale" is actually inappropriate for these creatures. They have never been known to attack anything other than their usual prey, and they are not whales—they are the largest member of the dolphin family.) About eighty-five orcas in three pods are resident in the San Juans spring to fall. These whales are very social and hunt salmon cooperatively. Each pod consists of related females and their young, accompanied by one or two unrelated bull males who are easily recognized by their size and towering dorsal fin. During summer, the pods sometimes come together to form a "superpod," in which the males of one pod mate with the females of another. The whales are most active during the mating season and are often seen breaching and spyhopping—much to the delight of whale-watchers. Unfortunately, the San Juan resident orca population has declined in recent years, a trend that hopefully can be reversed.

Nonresident orcas, called "transients," appear in the San Juans year-round. Quite different from their cousins who live in pods, transients live alone or in small family groups of two to three. They hunt seals and other marine mammals instead of salmon. The whales that live in pods are very noisy, using sound to communicate. Transients, on the other hand, are very quiet, presumably so they don't alert their prey.

In addition to orcas, a variety of other marine mammals live in or travel through the channels and inlets of the San Juans. Harbor seals, the most common, are frequently seen cruising through the water or resting on exposed rocks. One named "Popeye" hangs around the seafood dock in Friday Harbor and has trained the tourists to feed him. Sea lions, much larger than harbor seals, migrate through the islands to and from their breeding beaches in Alaska. Several minke whales live here, and the odd gray whale shows up during migration. Dall's porpoises, resembling small orcas, feed in the eddylines of open water and sometimes play in the bow wake of boats. River otters and mink live along the shorelines and forage for crabs and shellfish in shallow water.

Wild turkey

Below the surface, an amazing menagerie of creatures attracts divers from around the world. The giant octopus is the most famous of these, but there are many others that often defy imagination, such as many-armed sea stars two feet in diameter, big white anemones that look like cauliflower heads atop tall stalks, and the wizened wolf-eel, which grows to over ten feet long and eats urchins. The marine plant life is equally amazing. Beds of bull kelp dot the waters, growing from rocky bottom to the surface. Stands of eelgrass form tall prairies on sandy bottoms, creating important nurseries for juvenile fish, including salmon.

Seeing most of this marine life requires at least a wet suit and snorkeling gear, which you can rent at local dive shops. However, some of these unusual creatures are revealed at low tide, when viewing them requires nothing more than a pair of tall rubber boots. Pasted on the exposed rocks, purple sea stars, limpets, barnacles, and other species await the water's return. Tidepools resembling miniature aquariums teem with small crabs, green sea anemones, pink coralline algae, and other curiosities. Even the patches of crab-clawed rockweed are alive with tiny crabs and colorful shellfish.

Humans have been part of the islands' ecosystem for at least 9,000 years. Tribes of the southern Coast Salish lived in the San Juans for centuries prior to the arrival of Europeans. The Lummi, the predominant tribe, shared the islands with the Samish, Saanich, and Songish tribes. Archaeologists have found evidence of more than 280 settlements on San Juan Island alone, including a massive longhouse nearly 600 feet in length on the shore of Garrison Bay. These early inhabitants caught salmon in the open water, gathered shellfish in the intertidal zone, and foraged in the uplands. Facilitated by a common language and large canoes, the Salish tribes traded extensively among themselves, developing a relatively peaceful culture. Other tribes, such as the Kwakwa̱ka̱'wakw and Haida, visited the islands to trade with, and sometimes raid, the resident Salish.

Beach pebbles and driftwood

Europeans first came to the San Juans in 1791, when a boat from the Spanish expedition led by Francisco Eliza circled the islands. Eliza named the archipelago after the Viceroy of Mexico. The next year, the Spanish returned to explore further and unexpectedly encountered a larger British expedition led by George Vancouver. The Spanish accepted Vancouver's offer to collaborate on charting the area. The legacy of this collaboration and the early Spanish explorers remains in the names of many of the archipelago's islands and channels, such as San Juan, Orcas, Lopez, Haro, and Rosario. Faced with bigger threats elsewhere, the Spanish abandoned the area soon after, leaving it to the British, who claimed the entire region as part of their empire.

In 1846, the 49th parallel was established as the boundary between the expanding United States and the British territory. Unfortunately, the wording of the treaty left the ownership of the San Juan Islands in doubt. The British regarded Rosario Strait, east of the San Juans, as the boundary and thus claimed ownership. The Americans, however, regarded Haro Strait, to the west, as the boundary and so also claimed the archipelago. Thus an otherwise insignificant cluster of islands became the stage for a clash between the aging British Empire and its upstart offspring.

Using their well-established position at Fort Victoria on Vancouver Island, the British gained control in the early 1850s by chartering the Hudson's Bay Company to colonize the islands. The Company built a significant farming and fishing operation under the protective shield of the British Navy. Meanwhile, the American government sent an expedition to map the area, and a handful of American settlers staked claims. Both sides expanded their presence throughout the 1850s, regarding each other as illegal squatters and periodically threatening each other with force. Except for a few minor skirmishes, however, neither side had the firepower or willpower to actually confront the other.

Tensions peaked in 1859 in what has become known as the Pig War, the last armed conflict between the United States and Britain. Fortunately, the only casualty was a Hudson's Bay Company pig, which had rooted in American settler Lyman Cutler's potato patch one time too many. To protect their citizens, both nations sent in more military firepower, with the two sides facing off near Cattle Point on San Juan Island. Fortunately, cooler heads prevailed and the crisis was averted. The two sides agreed to joint occupation until the dispute could be resolved. Finally, in 1872, Kaiser Wilhelm of Germany settled the argument in favor of the United States, setting the boundary through Boundary Pass and Haro Strait. Today, the legacy of the Pig War lives on at American Camp and English Camp, both part of the San Juan Island National Historic Park.

Out of the spotlight of international conflict, the San Juans returned to being a rural backwater in a remote corner of the nation. For the next hundred years, the islands attracted little attention and the small population grew slowly. Islanders made their living by fishing, farming, building boats, logging, and producing lime. Another trade—smuggling—has a long tradition in the San Juans. Through the years, colorful and sometimes ruthless characters such as "Pig Iron" Kelly have smuggled in Chinese railroad workers, Canadian wool, booze during Prohibition, and more recently, drugs.

The boat building, logging, and lime works are long gone. Commercial fishers continue to take salmon, but far fewer than the millions caught in the late 1800s and early 1900s. Today most commercial boats catch Dungeness crab, shrimp, sea cucumber, and sea urchin. The occasional smuggler still slips across the border with illegal drugs, immigrants, or even Cuban cigars. Farming is still a big part of island life, defining much of the rural character of the islands.

Today people come to the San Juans from all over the world to escape the mainland's pressures and enjoy the islands' slow pace, scenery, and outdoor recreation. The islands' orcas and protected waters are among the main attractions, but there are also sophisticated art galleries, quaint B&Bs, scenic bike rides, and award-winning wineries. Some visitors stay only a few days, but an increasing number return frequently or simply never leave. Most people come to San Juan, Orcas, Lopez, and Shaw, the largest islands and the only ones served by the Washington State ferries. Some of the smaller islands can be visited by water taxi or private boat, but most are privately owned or protected as preserves.

San Juan, the second largest island, is the most populous, with more than 5,000 residents. The archipelago's only incorporated town and its county seat, Friday Harbor, is located on the east side on a well-protected harbor of the same name. The town is a popular tourist destination and a bustling community with plenty of good restaurants, hotels, art galleries, gift shops, and the islands' only brew pub. The harbor has a working port where the whale-watching fleet docks and commercial fishers bring their catches.

Legend has it that Friday Harbor was named when a ship entered the harbor in a thick fog. Seeing a man on the shore, someone on the ship inquired, "What bay is this?" "Friday" was the response. More likely, Friday Harbor was named for Joseph Pa'ilie, a Hawaiian sheepherder employed by the Hudson's Bay Company. Joseph, whom everyone called "Joe Friday," grazed his flocks on the harbor's grassy banks. Thus the harbor became known as Joe Friday's Harbor, later shortened to the current name.

Outside of town, San Juan Island is a patchwork of open prairies, pastures, second-growth forests, and residences. The island's southern end consists of largely open, rolling prairie, which turns golden brown in the dry summers. You often can see fox, which live only on San Juan Island, and their prey, the rabbits descended from those raised by early settlers. Inland and north, San Juan becomes more hilly and forested. Cattle, horses, llamas, and alpacas graze in the pastures, and several lakes provide excellent bass and trout fishing. Lime Kiln Point, on the island's west side, is the site of an old lighthouse and the country's only whale-watching park. During the summer, orcas often thrill visitors by swimming just off the park's rocky shore. Roche Harbor, on the northern end, is a well-protected harbor with a marina and historic resort.

Orcas, the largest of the San Juan Islands, is second in population, with about 3,500 residents. It is a heavily wooded, almost mountainous, horseshoe-shaped island. Mount Constitution and the lesser peaks in Moran State Park occupy the eastern side of the horseshoe. As you hike among the big trees or paddle the pristine lakes that dot the park's valleys, you feel as though you are in the mountains rather than on a coastal island.

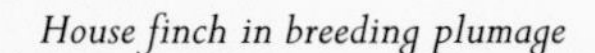

House finch in breeding plumage

The village of Eastsound, the island's business center and home to a handful of shops, inns, and restaurants, sits at the head of East Sound, at the apex of the horseshoe. On the horseshoe's west side, the rounded bulge of aptly named Turtleback Mountain looms over the pastures and orchards of Crow Valley as well as over the bays of West Sound and Deer Harbor. The head of West Sound, called Massacre Bay, was a major site used by the Lummi tribe prior to the arrival of Europeans. Legend has it that a band of Haidas killed most of the Lummis in a surprise attack; hence the bay's name. The Lummis retreated from Orcas Island to the mainland and to what is now called Lummi Island, east of Orcas.

Lopez, the third largest island, is home to about 2,000 residents and even more sheep. In contrast to Orcas's mountains, Lopez has open, gently rolling terrain, making it a popular destination for bicyclists. Lopez Village, on Fisherman Bay, serves as the island's commercial center, with the rest of the island a patchwork of second-growth forest and working farms that produce cattle, sheep, truck crops, and even grapes for the island's winery.

Lopez's puzzle-piece shape results from the islands' many tombolos—narrow spits formed by sediment deposited between two islands. Fisherman Bay and Sperry Peninsula were formed by tombolos that connected Lopez to former islands. Spencer Spit is a tombolo that reaches for Frost Island, but a strong current keeps them from touching.

The San Juans have that friendliness you expect of small, rural places. However, the Lopezians, as they call themselves, seem to be the friendliest of all. They wave to everyone who passes by, pick up hitchhikers, and will sometimes lead you to your destination when you ask for directions. Several of the island's farmers simply place eggs, jams, or produce by the road with a "For Sale" sign, trusting their customers to leave the right amount in the money box.

Shaw Island is the smallest of the state ferry-served islands. A heavily wooded island surrounded by its three bigger siblings, Shaw is best known for its solitude and for the nuns that run the ferry landing and the island's only store. Two orders of nuns, an order of monks, and a few hundred other people make Shaw their home. With no restaurants or lodgings, the island receives few visitors. But Blind Bay, on the north side, is one of the San Juan's best anchorages, and the county park on the south side has an excellent campground and beach.

None of the other islands is served by the ferry system, yet people live on many of them. Most have little public access and few amenities for visitors. A few hundred self-sufficient residents determined to preserve the last island frontier live on Waldron, northwest of Orcas. They grow or make most of what they need and even have a one-room schoolhouse. Northeast of San Juan Island, Spieden Island is home to a few people and a large herd of exotic ungulates left over from its days as "Safari Island." The then-owners stocked the island with game from Africa and Asia, and marketed safaris to well-heeled hunters. The operation went bust after a few years, leaving many of the animals behind. Nearby Stuart Island, with a number of permanent and seasonal residents, is bisected by a state park that is a popular boating destination. The county road leads to an old lighthouse on the north end. Along the way, you pass the island's schoolhouse, where islanders keep a water cooler with paper cups for people and a dish for dogs.

A number of other islands are state parks, accessible only by private boat. Three of these, Matia, Sucia, and Patos, line the northeastern corner of the archipelago. Their yellowish rock, not found elsewhere in the San Juans, has been sculpted by wave action into sometimes surprising shapes. An old lighthouse on the northern tip of Patos stands watch over the archipelago's junction with the Strait of Georgia and Canadian waters. Jones Island, another state park, is home to several nearly-tame deer, which are always a big hit with visiting kids. Just off the northeast corner of San Juan, Turn Island often hosts a nesting pair of bald eagles. Many of these islands are part of the Cascadia Marine Trail, with campsites reserved for kayakers.

The remaining islands are either publicly or privately owned, with little or no development or public access. Most are protected as preserves or as part of the San Juan Island National Wildlife Refuge. People are required to stay at least a hundred yards away to avoid disturbing the wildlife. Yellow Island, a preserve owned by The Nature Conservancy, is one of the few that individuals or small groups can visit. Each spring, wildflowers turn the island into a showy palette of color, usually peaking around Mother's Day.

The San Juan Islands are a very special place, but are in danger of being loved to death. Currently, they are experiencing a surge of growth and popularity. Some islanders refer to this as a renaissance; others aren't so sure. But for good or bad, the influx of tourists, retirees, and seasonal residents is changing the islands. Hopefully, the San Juans will still be a magic place for the next generation of residents and visitors.

A cruise on a Washington State Ferry provides passage to the San Juan Islands as well as a relaxing way to see their beauty on a sunny summer day.

Left: *Farming is still a significant part of life in the San Juan Islands. Hay bales dot the landscape in summer and feed livestock in winter.*

Right: *At a lush garden on Lopez Island, a colorful scarecrow frightens the birds away and a tall fence keeps out the deer.*

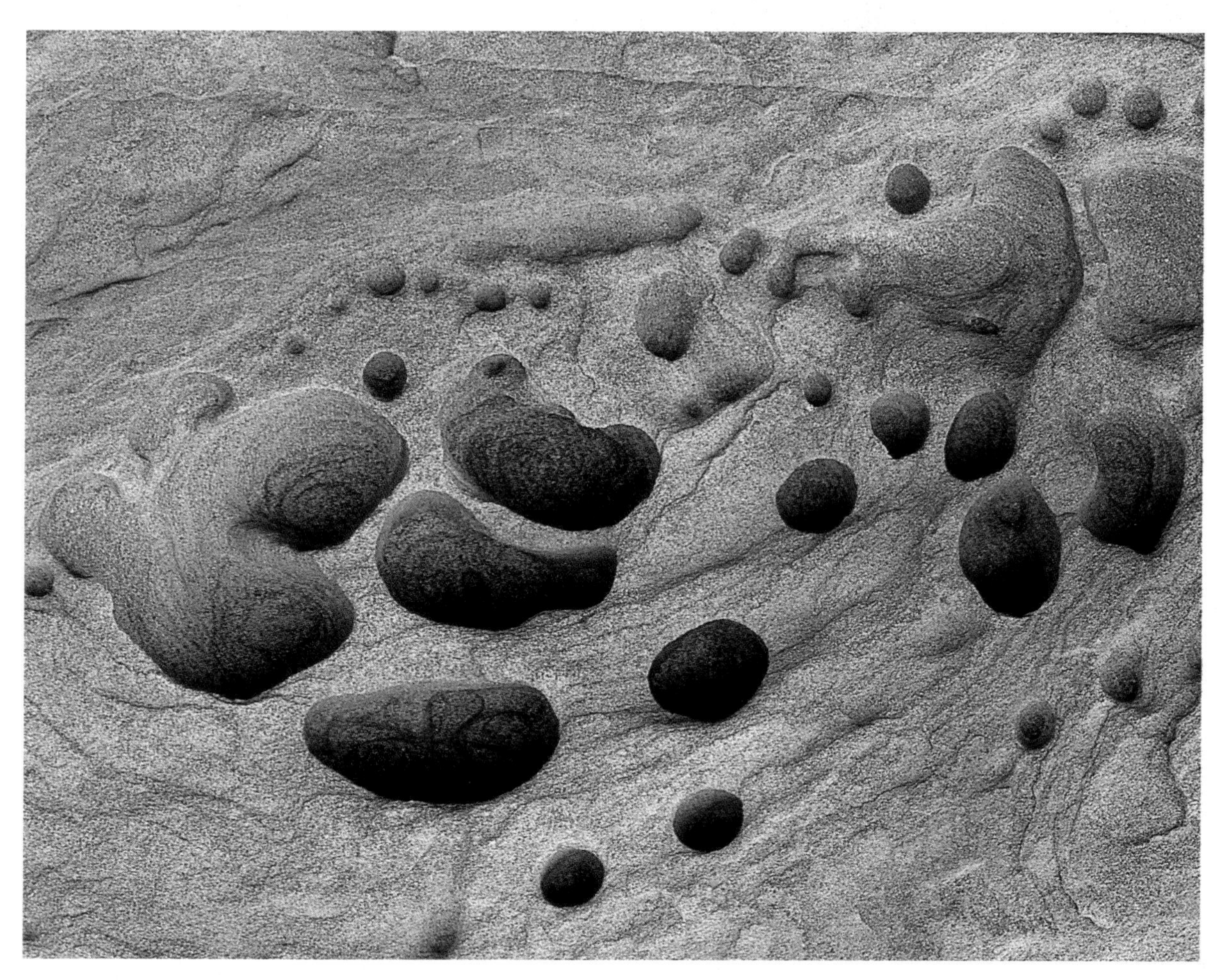

Left: *The sculpted rocks of Sucia Island and Ewing Island frame Mount Baker in the distance.*

Above: *Erosion exposes small rocks embedded in Sucia Island's sandstone, creating unusual and distinctive patterns.*

***Left**: The colorful Pacific madrona grows throughout the San Juans. This unusual tree loses its bark in summer but keeps its leathery leaves in winter.*

***Right**: A tiny Pacific tree frog, also known as the Pacific chorus frog, uses the peeling bark of a madrona tree as a perch.*

***Far right**: Baked by sun, the red bark of a madrona splits and curls to reveal the soft, green wood underneath.*

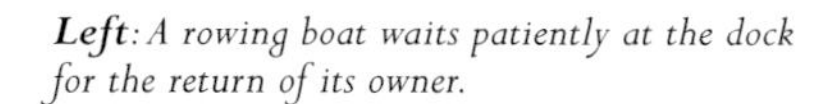

***Left**: A rowing boat waits patiently at the dock for the return of its owner.*

***Right**: Commercial fishing is a small but important component of island life. These crab pots are used to catch the tasty Dungeness crab.*

***Below**: With the reduction in local salmon populations over the past decade, fishing nets remain piled on the dock for much of the year.*

The rising sun breaks through the mist and clouds at Peavine Pass, Blakely Island.

The San Juans are a popular boating destination, especially during the summer months. These visiting Grand Banks trawlers line the docks at Friday Harbor during an owners' rendezvous.

A commercial gillnet boat lies moored in Fisherman Bay on Lopez. With today's shortened fishing seasons, the San Juan fleet has dwindled to a handful.

Grasses and teasels, which are non-native, fill the golden prairies that dominate the south-facing slopes of San Juan Island.

***Far left**: Songbirds that feed on seeds, like this American goldfinch, are abundant in the islands' prairies and thickets.*

***Below left:** Early settlers and the Hudson's Bay Company brought rabbits to the islands in the mid-1800s, raising them for food. The descendents of those rabbits are now common on the larger islands.*

***Right**: A profusion of spring wildflowers, including buttercup, death camas, and blue camas, bloom around an old split-rail fence at American Camp on San Juan Island.*

Above: *For several weeks each May, a colorful palette of blooming wildflowers, like these paintbrush, blue camas, and buttercup, covers Yellow Island.*

Right: *Blue camas and chocolate lilies on Yellow Island.*

A flower-filled knoll overlooks the caretaker's cabin on Yellow Island, a preserve owned by The Nature Conservancy.

Left: *Large boulders left by glaciers line the beach on Clark Island. Little Sister Island, part of the extensive San Juan Islands National Wildlife Refuge, lies beyond.*

Right: *Small- to medium-sized beach cobbles cover most of the islands' beaches.*

Lower right: *Erosion, primarily caused by chemical interaction between the sandstone and seawater, creates interesting honeycomb patterns where embedded rocks have been dislodged from the eroding sandstone.*

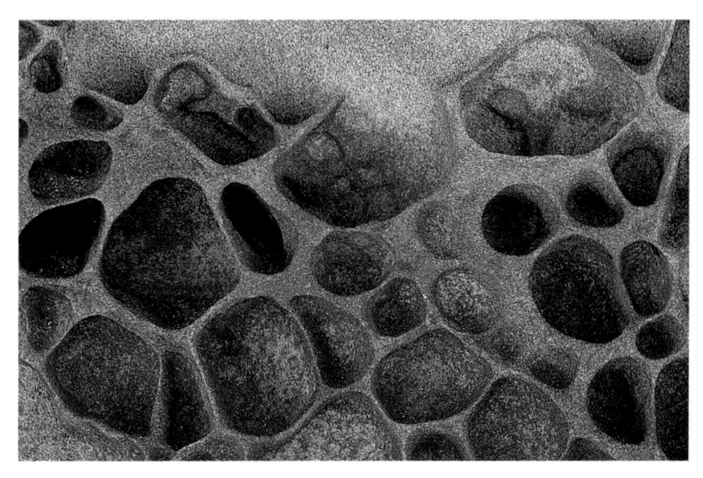

Harbor seals, the most common marine mammal in the San Juans, bask on Whale Rocks, south of Lopez Island. Cattle Point, at the tip of San Juan Island, lies beyond.

A golden wave of sculpted sandstone on one of the Cluster Islets seems to break over Orcas Island in the distance.

Bull kelp fills the waters around Iceberg Point on Lopez Island, at the very southern end of the archipelago.

Mount Baker looms over the old lighthouse at Alden Point on Patos Island, at the very northern end of the archipelago.

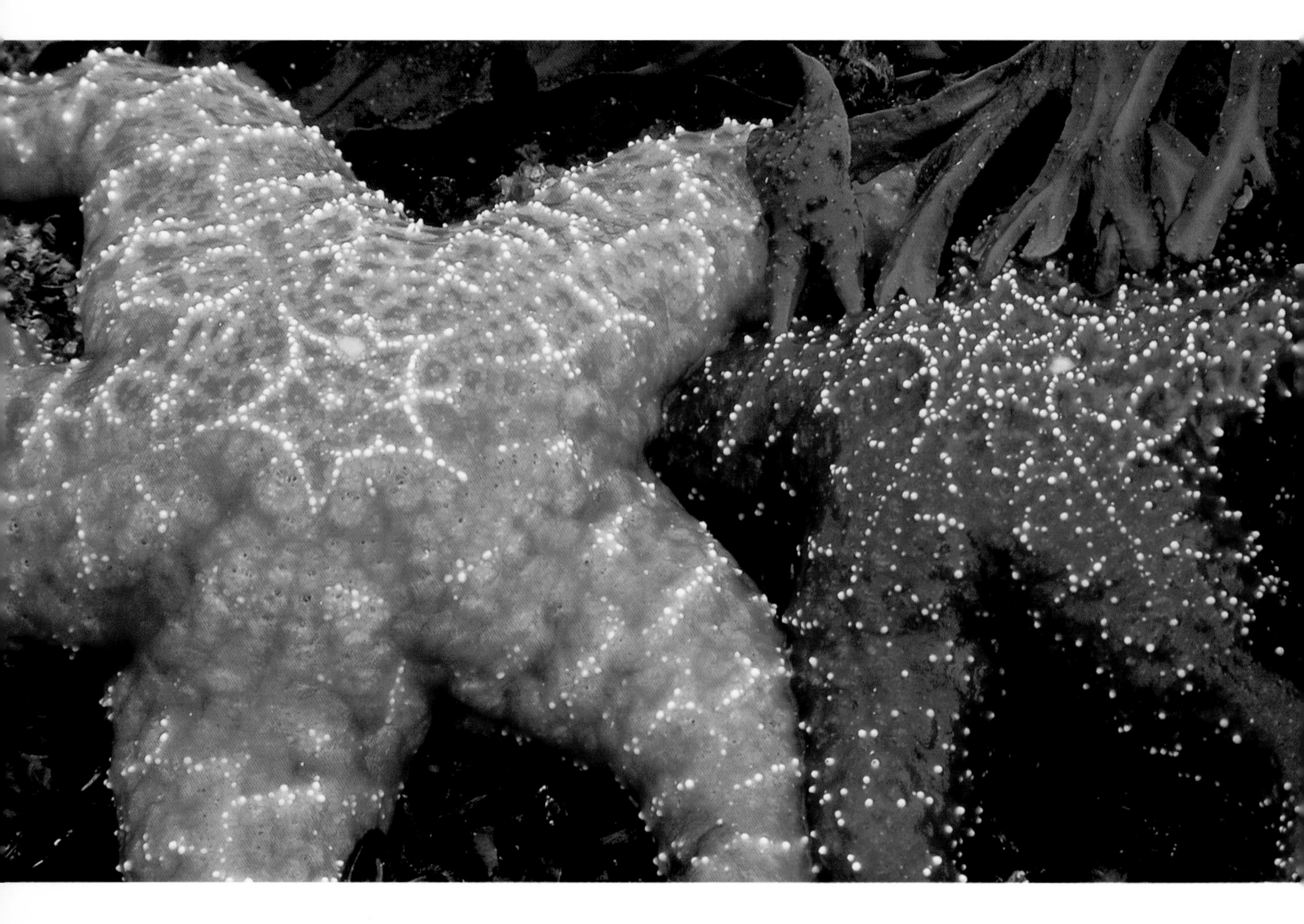

Ochre sea stars and a menagerie of other colorful creatures are revealed at low tide along the islands' rocky shorelines.

Above: *The swollen tips of rockweed, which grows on rocks exposed at low tide, resemble crab claws.*

Right: *Small green sea anemones and other curiosities fill the pools left when the tide recedes.*

Kids explore the rocks at low tide along Agate Beach on Lopez Island.

The historic resort at Roche Harbor, at the northern end of San Juan Island, is one of the islands' more popular destinations.

THOMAS
GRAHAM
DIED
May 18. 1892

Mist shrouds the gravestones in the old cemetery across from Center Church on Lopez Island.

Rustic Falls is one of several waterfalls along Cascade Creek, which flows through the forest on Mount Constitution's southern flank on Orcas Island.

The forest at the Shark Reef Recreation Area on Lopez Island provides a quiet sanctuary for hikers and wildlife.

109
27696

Left: *Billowing spinnakers drive sailboats at the Shaw Island Classic, the San Juan Islands' premier sailing event.*

Right: *A more relaxed sailor barbecues dinner at a quiet anchorage in Blind Bay, Shaw Island.*

Early morning mist rises as swallows swoop over Hummel Lake, on Lopez Island.

Visitors search for orcas at Lime Kiln Point State Park on San Juan Island, the country's only whale-watching park.

The light at Cattle Point, on the southeastern tip of San Juan Island, guides boaters through tricky Cattle Pass into San Juan Channel.

LOOKSHA IV
LOOKSHA IV

Colorful kayaks line the shore at Fisherman Bay, Lopez Island.

American Camp, used by the U.S. Army during its occupation of San Juan Island from 1859 to 1872, is now part of the San Juan Island National Historic Park.

A curious red fox kit explores the area around his den while his mother is away hunting. Fox are common on San Juan Island, but absent on the other islands.

A kayak provides an intimate view of a surfacing orca.

Left: *As one orca surfaces to breathe, another is upside down slapping its tail on the surface.*

Below: *Mature males, or bulls, are recognizable by their impressively tall dorsal fin and larger size.*

The town of Friday Harbor hosts a holiday decorations contest during the Christmas season. Santa waves from his boat atop a local restaurant.

The Post San Juan building twinkles brightly at the north end of town.

Left: *Drift logs line the beach at the head of Spencer Spit on Lopez Island. The spit reaches toward Frost Island in the background.*

Right: *The inter-island ferry passes Upright Head on Lopez Island during an early morning run.*

Left: *Orcas Landing sits quietly in the rain, awaiting the arrival of the next ferry.*

Right: *A ferry enters the San Juan archipelago through Thatcher Pass, between Blakely and Decatur Islands.*

California poppies bloom in fields and along roadsides during the summer.

Left: *Shooting stars are among the earliest wild-flowers to emerge in spring.*

Above: *The fairyslipper is a showy orchid that decorates the forest floor throughout the islands.*

The steep cliffs and old lighthouse at Turn Point on Stuart Island mark the northwestern corner of the archipelago.

Right: *A rhinoceros auklet, often seen in the open waters of the San Juans, surfaces from a dive.*

Below: *A black oystercatcher searches exposed rockweed for a hidden meal.*

Rocks covered by orange lichen frame South Beach on San Juan Island, the longest beach in the archipelago.

A lone paddler enjoys a summer sunset.

Left: *Speiden Island is home to a large herd of exotic animals, left from its days as Safari Island.*

Right: *A driftwood bench provides a quiet spot to relax on Orcas Island.*

Dusk casts a somber light over Griffin Bay and San Juan Island.

Mark Gardner is a professional photographer who lives on San Juan Island. For years he has roamed all over the San Juan Islands by car, kayak, bicycle, foot, and boat, taking photographs. A variety of editorial and commercial clients have published his images, and he is the author, with Art Wolfe, of *Photography Outdoors: A Field Guide for Travel & Adventure Photographers*. Gardner can be contacted at mark@rainshadow-arts.com or through his Web site, www.rainshadow-arts.com, where you can see additional island images.

Royalties from the sales of this book will be donated to the Friends of the San Juans, a nonprofit organization with the mission "to protect and promote the health and future of the San Juan Islands." With over a thousand memberships, Friends works to protect the natural beauty and ecological integrity of the islands, as well as the sociological and economic diversity of the rural communities that make up the San Juans. Thus, your purchase of this book helps protect this unique archipelago. For more information about Friends of the San Juans, call 360-378-2319 or visit their Web site at www.sanjuans.org.